Contents

DID YOU KNOW?

For parents and children accustomed to long, time-consuming tests, it may seem impossible to truly gather sufficient placement information with just a few questions. But, the truth is that you can easily and effectively learn where to place your child academically in a subject with just twenty simple questions!

How is this possible? Well, keep in mind that most achievement tests are administered to large groups of students, and the results are processed through computers. Therefore, these tests require a minimum of three to five questions per topic in order to assess an average.

When a test is administered one on one and the parent walks through each question with their child, however, the assessment results are not strictly based on right or wrong answers. Instead, they are based on observation of thought processes, understanding of the question, and the ability to work through the question or problem. As a result, typically only one question, combined with interactive administration of the test, is required to adequately assess a child's level of understanding.

Well Planned Start includes both the administrator guide and step-by-step answer key in order for parents to confidently administer, observe, and evaluate the test-taking process to understand exactly where their children place.

A TOOL FOR PARENTS

As a mom of five, I began giving my kids achievement tests at an early age. After teaching them how to fill in the small circles and sharpen their number 2 pencils, the kids would walk into classrooms, doors would close, and testing would begin. Six weeks later, I would receive test reports which gave vague indications of how each child was doing compared to children across the nation. The broad descriptions of achievement in specific areas provided very little useful information to help me know how to strengthen my kids in the coming year.

Over the years, I sought an assessment option that would help me choose the best curriculum, cover information unknown to my child, and fill in any educational gaps. Unfortunately, none of the tests I found accomplished this goal. That needed to change!

Recognizing the need, I began working with the Well Planned Gal curriculum developer **Tiffany Orthman, M.Ed.** to develop a one-of-a-kind, easy-to-use assessment and placement test for parents and children to work through together.

Well Planned Start is unique as it guides you, the parent, to a better understanding of what your child knows, comprehends, and can process correctly. This educational evaluation tool offers a two-sided assessment. First, you will find a parent assessment, helping you discover what you know about your child. Second, a student placement test walks your child through a series of questions while you follow along with an administrator guide that helps you know how to process your child's answers and thinking processes.

Best of all, I've included helpful tips for each of the subjects and areas, as well as a checklist of milestones for this school year. Milestones work as a guide as you watch your child develop emotionally, physically, and educationally throughout the year.

As you proceed through this book and into your school year, remember these five key points:

- Relax! This is not a comparison or a judgment game. This is a tool to help you determine where your child is.

- Use the information to make improvements. Spend extra time or use a different approach where there are weaknesses. Offer more activities if you need to challenge your child. If you have not covered an area, now is the time!

- Try to set aside presuppositions as you begin the assessment. Remember, dislike for a subject does not indicate a weakness.

- These assessments are based on grasping concepts rather than parroting correct answers.

- Bible has been added as an additional component in these assessments. Keep in mind, though, that spiritual growth is not based on age. This is simply a resource to help you have an idea of where to look for and encourage growth.

Rebecca Farris
WELL PLANNED GAL

BOOK OVERVIEW

The Well Planned Start has been organized and arranged in order of sequence. Each section has an introduction with detailed information on how to assess your child, administer the placement test, and understand the milestones.

PARENT ASSESSMENT TESTS

The goal of this section is to become familiar with what your child knows. If your child has been attending school or hybrid home-schooling, this area will give you the opportunity to begin dialogues to understand the depth of understanding in each subject.

There are detailed instructions on how to use this assessment, as well as worksheets to journal your findings. At the end of this section, we give practical teaching tips to help you enhance each subject area.

STUDENT PLACEMENT TESTS

Unlike standardized testing, these placement tests allow parents to see first hand the specific areas children excel and need help in. By using the guide to administer the tests, you not only give instructions to your child, but you will also follow instructions that help you know what to watch for as the child works through the questions. This allows you to discover where the breakdown begins in the process.

PARENT TEACHING TIPS

After administering tests, you will find practical teaching tips and activity suggestions for every concept covered in the placement test. Use these suggested activities to strengthen low-scoring areas, keep your child challenged, fill in gaps, and more!

5TH GRADE MILESTONES

Complete with a checklist of milestones, Well Planned Start provides a year-long guide on what to expect from your child physically, emotionally, and academically. Beyond what they should achieve, we've included what they may achieve, including even advanced achievements. An additional checklist is included in each area to let you know how to help your child along the way.

TESTING OBSTACLES

If your child has never taken a test before or has trouble when testing, the Well Planned Start assessments offer a great introduction to testing and are relaxed enough to put any child at ease.

The assessments are not timed, and there are no little circles on separate sheets of paper that children have to navigate. Instead, parents are encouraged to engage children, review instructions, or stop for a break when needed.

In the comfort of your home and with the assurance of a parent administering the assessment, children working through Well Planned Start are able to relax, comprehend, access the information, and enjoy the experience.

Well Planned Start ensures an accurate and enjoyable assessment and placement for children and parents.

#1 START HERE

Begin with the Parent Assessment

PARENT ASSESSMENT

The following pages contain the parent assessment tests for math, language arts, history & geography, science, and Bible. Use this section to begin understanding what your child should know and comprehend. Here are a few tips as you proceed through the questions ahead:

- If you are unsure about the questions and answers, do a quick Internet search.

- If you are unsure whether a topic has been or will be covered, do a little digging. Speak to a representative at your child's previous school or take a quick look through your past or current homeschool curriculum.

- Engage your child in a discussion to see how deep his or her knowledge is. Remembering the significance of an event is more important than knowing a date for a test.

- Try to figure things out together. This is a team effort.

- Lack of information does not necessarily indicate a gap. For example, if you have not covered early American history yet but are sure your child would understand it, give your child credit for abilities.

- Watch your child's general attitude toward learning. If there is a lot of negativity, plan to take a step back to regain a love of learning.

- As you process through this assessment with your child, go with your gut instinct. If you feel your child is good at something, say so. If you feel he or she is struggling, say so.

- Think back to all the times you observed your child doing school work, playing, or having conversations. Do you feel that he or she understands the concepts?

- If you don't feel confident in your knowledge, ask for help from family and friends.

- Ask classmates, former teachers, or other homeschool moms what their observations of your child are.

- Be sure that you administer the entire assessment. If your assessment and your child's performance do not match up, investigate possible causes such as test anxiety or lack of information.

BEYOND ACADEMICS

Well Planned Start offers a great baseline for assessing grade placement and academic, emotional, and physical progress. But, be sure to remember your child's need to explore interests as well.

During 5th grade, you will see a narrowing of your child's interests from the wide exploration of the early elementary years as specific hobbies and activities become more appealing. Your child may progress to a more experienced level in skills begun in younger years, or this may be the year that groundwork is laid for interests that will develop further in high school.

Because academics begin to take more time during these middle school years, be proactive about preserving two to three opportunities a week specifically for pursuit and development of interests.

WHOLE NUMBERS TO THE BILLIONS

	YES	NO

Can your child read and write numbers to the billions? ○ ○

Does your child understand prime numbers? ○ ○
*A prime number is a whole number greater than 1,
whose only two whole-number factors are 1 and itself.*

Is your child able to find the greatest common factor of a number? ○ ○
The highest number that divides exactly into two or more numbers.

Can your child find the least common multiple of given numbers? ○ ○
The smallest positive number that is a multiple of two or more numbers.

RATIO AND PERCENT

	YES	NO

Can your child express simple ratios? ○ ○
*A ratio says how much of one thing there is
compared to another thing.*

Is your child able to make scale drawings? ○ ○

Can your child calculate the percent of a number? ○ ○

Is your child able to figure fraction,
decimal, and percent equivalents? $\frac{1}{8} = .125$ ○ ○

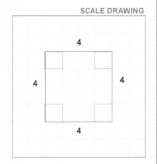

SCALE DRAWING

FRACTIONS AND DECIMALS

	YES	NO

Can your child find the least common denominator of fractions? ○ ○

Is your child able to put fractions in lowest terms? $\frac{6}{9} = \frac{2}{3}$ ○ ○

Can your child add, subtract, multiply, and divide with decimals? ○ ○

Is your child able to round decimals? ○ ○

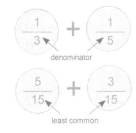

$\frac{1}{3} + \frac{1}{5}$

denominator

$\frac{5}{15} + \frac{3}{15}$

least common

MULTIPLICATION AND DIVISION

	YES	NO

Can your child multiply by 4-digit numbers? ○ ○

Is your child able to divide by 3-digit numbers? ○ ○

Can your child estimate multiplication and division problems? ○ ○

Is your child able to solve multi-step word problems? ○ ○

GEOMETRY

	YES	NO

Can your child measure and draw angles and line segments? ○ ○

Is your child able to identify types of triangles? ○ ○

Can your child find the area of irregular shapes? ○ ○

Is your child able to find the volume and surface area of a box? ○ ○
*Volume = (h)(w)(l)
Surface Area = 2(hw) + 2(hl) + 2(wl)*

5th - 8th grade
BEGINNING TO UNDERSTAND
MATH

What was a subject full of fact memorization in the early years becomes much more practical in this stage of learning. Even children who have disliked math can grow to enjoy it as they see how ratios, fractions, and geometry apply to real life.

Encourage your child to help alter recipes or figure sales tax on a shopping trip to see math in real life action!

Language Arts

An antecedent is the word (or words) that a pronoun refers to.

COMMA , COLON :

Alliteration is when you use words that have the same sound at the beginning.

Onomatopoeia is a word which imitates the natural sounds of a thing.

5th - 8th grade
BEGINNING TO UNDERSTAND
LANGUAGE ARTS

As with math, components of grammar should solidify during these middle school years as your child begins to implement all of those isolated concepts learned in the early years.

This is the perfect time to work on writing skills and show the reason for learning about punctuation and parts of speech. Make it fun by creating silly stories and poems!

WRITING   YES   NO

Does your child write reports, summaries, letters, descriptions, essays, stories, and poems?   ○   ○

Can your child organize, draft, revise, and proofread independently?   ○   ○

Is your child able to direct a piece of writing toward an audience?   ○   ○

Can your child write well-organized paragraphs?   ○   ○

RESEARCH   YES   NO

Can your child use an atlas?   ○   ○
An atlas is a collection of various maps of the earth or a specific region of the earth, such as the U.S. or Europe. The maps in atlases show geographic features and the topography of an area's landscape.

Is your child able to do Internet research?   ○   ○

Does your child use research to support his or her writing?   ○   ○

Can your child write a bibliography?   ○   ○
A bibliography is a list of all of the sources you have used in the process of researching your work.

SPELLING AND VOCABULARY   YES   NO

Does your child consistently use new words when writing and speaking?   ○   ○

Does your child consult the dictionary on a regular basis?   ○   ○

Can your child use knowledge of prefixes, base words, and suffixes to spell unfamiliar words?   ○   ○

Is your child able to use a glossary?   ○   ○
Glossaries are collections of words and definitions that pertain to a particular subject.

GRAMMAR AND USAGE   YES   NO

Can your child correct sentence fragments and run-ons?   ○   ○

Does your child correctly use nouns, pronouns, verbs, adjectives, adverbs, conjunctions, and interjections?   ○   ○

Is your child able to make pronouns and antecedents agree?   ○   ○

Can your child correctly use colons and commas?   ○   ○

LITERATURE   YES   NO

Can your child define alliteration, onomatopoeia, metaphor, and simile?   ○   ○

Does your child know what a tragedy, comedy, act, and scene are?   ○   ○

Is your child able to read plays?   ○   ○

Does your child read independently outside of school hours?   ○   ○

WORLD HISTORY

	YES	NO
Does your child know about the Maya, Inca, and Aztec civilizations?	○	○
Can your child name reasons for exploration?	○	○
Is your child familiar with the Italian city-states?	○	○
Does your child know about Henry VIII and Elizabeth I?	○	○

WORLD GEOGRAPHY

	YES	NO
Can your child describe climate zones?	○	○
Is your child able to name lakes around the world?	○	○
Can your child locate countries around the world?	○	○
Is your child able to locate mountains around the world?	○	○

UNITED STATES HISTORY

	YES	NO
Does your child know who Daniel Boone was?	○	○
Can your child explain some of the events that led to the Civil War?	○	○
Is your child familiar with the Transcontinental Railroad?	○	○
Does your child know what Manifest Destiny is?	○	○

UNITED STATES GEOGRAPHY

	YES	NO
Can your child describe the different climates of the United States?	○	○
Can your child name U.S. regions?	○	○
Does your child know the states and capitals?	○	○
Is your child able to name major rivers in the U.S.?	○	○

CULTURE

	YES	NO
Is your child familiar with art from around the world?	○	○
Is your child able to match music with different countries?	○	○
Can your child name some holidays from around the world?	○	○
Does your child enjoy ethnic food?	○	○

History
& Geography

The Maya, Inca, and Aztecs built great civilizations in Mexico and in Central and South America between 1,800 and 500 years ago.

The Transcontinental Railroad was a 1,912-mile railroad line connecting the east with the west.

Manifest Destiny was a phrase which invoked the idea of divine sanction for the territorial expansion of the United States.

5th - 8th grade
BEGINNING TO UNDERSTAND
HISTORY & GEOGRAPHY

This stage stands as a strong bridge between the fun, general learning of the early years and the more targeted, reason-centered focus of high school.

This is a great time to utilize timelines and maps to show how various events in history intersect, laying the groundwork for the more idealogical lessons of the high school years.

Science

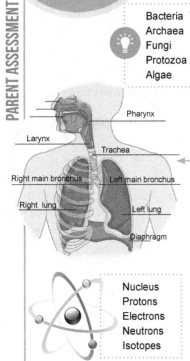

Bacteria
Archaea
Fungi
Protozoa
Algae

Pharynx
Larynx
Trachea
Right main bronchus
Left main bronchus
Right lung
Left lung
Diaphragm

Nucleus
Protons
Electrons
Neutrons
Isotopes

5th - 8th grade

BEGINNING TO UNDERSTAND

SCIENCE

Middle school offers the perfect opportunity to "get serious" about science. But, that doesn't mean it stops being fun!

Use these years to meld the hands-on exploration of early learning with some definite book facts. But, keep it hands on with fun, engaging experiments, models, and activities. Doing science is still the best way to learn.

10

LIVING THINGS   YES   NO

Does your child understand the five kingdoms?   ◯   ◯

Is your child able to name the characteristics of vertebrates?   ◯   ◯
Animals with an internal skeleton made of bone are called vertebrates.

Can your child name some single-celled organisms?   ◯   ◯

Does your child know the parts of a cell?   ◯   ◯

HUMAN BODY   YES   NO

Does your child understand the endocrine system?   ◯   ◯
The endocrine system is the collection of glands that produce hormones that regulate functions of the body.

Can your child explain the circulatory system?   ◯   ◯
The system that circulates blood and lymph through the body.

Is your child able to describe what the respiratory system does?   ◯   ◯

Does your child understand the effects of smoking and alcohol abuse?   ◯   ◯

PLANTS   YES   NO

Can your child tell you the difference between a vascular plant and a nonvascular plant?   ◯   ◯
Hint: Vascular plants have vessels to transport food, water, and xylem.

Is your child able to explain what photosynthesis does?   ◯   ◯

Does your child know what asexual plants, spore-bearing plants, nonflowering seed plants, and flowering plants are?   ◯   ◯

Can your child name the parts of a flower?   ◯   ◯

LIFE CYCLES   YES   NO

Is your child able to describe how bacteria reproduce?   ◯   ◯

Does your child understand how different animals reproduce? ◯   ◯

Can your child describe what regeneration is?   ◯   ◯
Hint: Lizards who lose all or part of their tails can grow new ones.

Is your child able to describe different growth stages of organisms?   ◯   ◯

CHEMISTRY   YES   NO

Does your child know the parts of an atom?   ◯   ◯

Can your child explain what an element is?   ◯   ◯
An element is a substance consisting of atoms which all have the same number of protons.

Is your child able to describe physical changes in substances?   ◯   ◯

Does your child understand what chemical change is?   ◯   ◯

Try this: mix baking soda and vinegar to produce carbon dioxide gas

BIBLE STORIES

	YES	NO
Is your child familiar with the Old Testament prophets?	○	○
Does your child know the story of Joseph?	○	○
Can your child name some events from Jesus' ministry?	○	○
Does your child know the story of Esther?	○	○

BIBLE REFERENCE TOOLS

	YES	NO
Does your child know how to use a Bible dictionary?	○	○
Does your child know how to use the concordance in a Bible?	○	○
Can your child use the maps at the back of a Bible?	○	○
Can your child find a passage without turning to the Table of Contents?	○	○

BIBLE PASSAGES

	YES	NO
Is your child familiar with Psalm 1? *Blessed is the man who walks not in the counsel of the wicked...*	○	○
Is your child familiar with Ephesians 4:29? *Let no corrupting talk come out of your mouths...*	○	○
Is your child familiar with the Romans Road?	○	○
Is your child familiar with John 1:7-10? *He came as a witness, to bear witness about the light, that all might believe through him...*	○	○

THEOLOGY

	YES	NO
Does your child understand atonement?	○	○
Does your child understand repentance?	○	○
Does your child know what a covenant is?	○	○
Does your child understand redemption?	○	○

CHURCH HISTORY & MISSIONS

	YES	NO
Does your child know who George Muller was?	○	○
Is your child familiar with George Whitefield?	○	○
Does your child know who William Carey was?	○	○
Is your child familiar with Amy Carmichael?	○	○

PROPHETS
Deborah
Samuel
Nathan
Elijah
Elisha
Huldah

Amy Carmichael: Missionary to India; founder of the Dohnavur Fellowship, a society devoted to saving neglected and ill-treated children

ATONEMENT
The reconciliation of God and mankind through the death of Jesus.

5ᵗʰ - 8ᵗʰ grade
BEGINNING TO UNDERSTAND
BIBLE

During these years, fun Bible stories give way to deeper concepts that will form the foundation for your child to hash out what he believes as he grows older.

Begin to introduce non-narrative portions of Scripture while also learning about the authors of each book of the Bible, how the Bible was compiled, and the history of the English translation.

MATH

Score	Section
	Whole Numbers to the Billions
	Ratio and Percents
	Fractions and Decimals
	Multiplication and Division
	Geometry

Total Score

Grade Placement

LANGUAGE ARTS

Score	Section
	Writing
	Research
	Spelling & Vocabulary
	Grammar & Usage
	Literature

Total Score

Grade Placement

HISTORY & GEOGRAPHY

Score	Section
	World History
	World Geography
	United States History
	United States Geography
	Culture

Total Score

Grade Placement

SCIENCE

Score	Section
	Living Things
	Human Body
	Plants
	Life Cycles
	Chemistry

Total Score

Grade Placement

BIBLE

Score	Section
	Bible Stories
	Bible Reference Tools
	Bible Passages
	Theology
	Church History and Missions

Total Score

Grade Placement

PARENT ASSESSMENT SCORING

The Well Planned Start was designed to assess a grade level *per subject.* Use the key below to *determine the grade level for each subject.*

1. Count the number of questions you answered yes to in each section. Write the number in the score box to the left of the section.

2. Add the section scores together and place the total in the **Total Score** box.

3. Using the key below, determine the grade assessment for *each subject.*

SUBJECT TEST KEY

- Total Score = 20: Administer the 6th grade test for this subject. Your child may be ready for 7th grade.
- Total Score = 15-19: Your child is ready for the 6th grade.
- Total Score = 10-14: Base your decision on the following **section scores.**
  - Score 2 or less in 1-2 sections: Your child is ready for the 6th grade in this subject, but you can expect to give extra help throughout the year.
  - Score 2 or less in 3-5 sections: Your child should begin this subject at a 5th grade level.
- All sections = 0-9: Administer the 4th grade test for this subject. Your child needs additional evaluation.

BIBLE EXCEPTION

Because the development of spiritual growth is not confined to a grade level, the Bible tests for Well Planned Start were designed to cover a range through the following stages of education:

- Starting Out - Preschool - 1st Grade
- Getting Excited: 2nd - 4th Grade
- Beginning to Understand: 5th - 8th Grade
- Learning to Reason: 9th - 12th Grade

When scoring Bible and determining placement, it is recommended to use your discretion in deciding if additional testing is needed or more time studying the topics covered.

WHAT NEXT?

The parent assessment is a guide to what key information your child should know by the end of the 5th grade. Once you have finished taking the assessment and scoring the results, you can proceed to give the student placement assessment to confirm your results.

Use this area to take notes about specific topics, subjects, and processes you feel your child will need help with. After your child has taken the placement test, compare your notes and the scores from the parent assessment to determine subject grades, overall grade level, and plan of action for the coming school year.

Assessment results can indicate grade levels below, at or above 5th grade. If you homeschool, you can purchase grade specific curriculum for each subject. However, if you are looking for a means to determine an overall grade level, use the suggestions below in deciding.

- If your child scores above or below a 5th grade level in math or language arts, you can easily incorporate materials from the assessed grade level. Your child should school in the 6th grade.

- If you child scores below a 5th grade level in three or more subjects (math, history, science, and language arts), we recommend repeating the 5th grade.

- If your child scores above a 5th grade level in three or more subjects (math, history, science, and language arts), we recommend testing with the 6th grade test for advanced placement.

- If your child scores ahead and behind in 2 or more subjects (math, history, science, and language arts), your child should school in the 6th grade.

- Reevaluate every year to be sure that your child is still at the correct grade.

#2 PROCEED

Proceed with Student Placement

STUDENT PLACEMENT TEST

The following pages contain the student placement tests for math, language arts, history and geography, science, and Bible. Along with the instructions on the test, there is also a section beginning on page 37 to reference as you watch your child work through the questions and answers. Utilizing this student placement test administrator guide will allow you to recognize the areas of struggle for your child and the point where problem solving breaks down.

The assessments ahead are a tool for you to use to better understand your child's academic needs. Here are a few more tips to use when administering these evaluations:

- Choose a calm day and a quiet space for assessment.

- Make sure your child is fresh and feeling well. Do not administer the assessments after three hours of calculus.

- Choose a time that is calm and fresh for you as well, as you will be working through the assessment with your child. It is important to minimize distractions for both you and your child during this time.

- Unless you have a child who enjoys tests and challenges, present these assessments as a new kind of activity or worksheet. If you say "test," they may lock up.

- Each assessment is printed on perforated pages. Simply remove each page and give it to the child to work on.

- Make sure your child understands the directions well.

- If the instructions are written in terms your child does not understand, feel free to change the wording.

- Take your time! These are not timed assessments. You are looking for correct thinking, not speed.

- As you process through this assessment with your child, go with your gut instinct. If you feel your child is good at something, say so. If you feel he or she is struggling, say so.

- Lack of information does not necessarily indicate a gap. For example, if you have not covered early American history yet but are sure your child would understand it, give your child credit for abilities.

- Look for creative thought processes. If you think an answer is weird, ask your child to explain how he or she arrived at it. If the logic behind the answer makes sense, give your child some credit.

- For concrete questions like math or science, watch for correct processes. Your child may be solving everything correctly and just writing down a wrong number or making a mistake in computation. If you are unsure, provide a new, similar problem for your child to work, or ask him to take another look. Having your child show his work will help.

- If you feel that there is a significant gap or that your child has not "gotten" the information after repeated exposure, please seek a professional evaluation for underlying issues. Whether you assign a label or not, understanding your child will make you a better teacher.

REMEMBER! ADMINISTRATOR GUIDE IS LOCATED BEHIND THE STUDENT TEST.

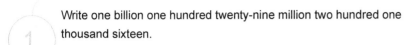

1. Write one billion one hundred twenty-nine million two hundred one thousand sixteen.

2. Circle the prime numbers below:

17   4   21   43

3. What is the greatest common factor of 81 and 117?

4. What is the least common multiple of 12 and 3?

5. If there are 18 girls and 24 boys in a class, what is the ratio of girls to boys?

6. Using a separate sheet of paper, draw a 12 ft. x 20 ft. room using a scale of 1 in.= 2 ft.

7. What is 55% of 75 to the nearest whole number?

8. What are the decimal and fraction equivalents of 96%?

9. What is the least common denominator of ¾ and ⁵⁄₆?

10. Put ²⁰⁄₃₅ in lowest terms.

11. $3.9 \div 300$

Math

12. What is 11.292016 rounded to the nearest tenth?

13.
$$4381$$
$$\times\ 8781$$

14. $81,432 \div 312$

15. Estimate: $4832 \div 5$

16. Mrs. Martin bought 3 dozen doughnuts for her family. If she has 4 children, how many doughnuts will each parent and child receive?

17. On a separate sheet of paper, draw a 1 in. line and a 3 in. line that meet at a 35 degree angle.

18. Find the area of this trapezoid:

6ft

8ft

10ft

19. What is the volume and surface area of this box?

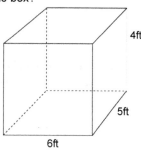

4ft

5ft

6ft

20. Draw a line to match the triangle with its type:

right-angle   acute   obtuse   scalene   isosceles   equilateral

16

Read this selection and write a summary.

1.

The ancient Greeks made a list of places they thought people should see. This list was named the Seven Wonders of the Ancient World. The Greeks chose seven wonders because in their culture this number symbolized perfection. The only one of the ancient wonders that still exists is in Giza, Egypt. This wonder is the Great Pyramid of Giza. It was one of three great pyramids built around 2500 B.C. It is the oldest wonder of the seven. People do not know how these pyramids were built but we know that they took over twenty years to complete. For a long time, the Great Pyramid was believed to be the tallest structure in the world. Pyramids were built as tombs for the leaders of Egypt called Pharaohs. Many travelers still visit the Great Pyramid today.

The Hanging Gardens of Babylon are another ancient wonder. This wonder is special because people do not know for sure if it existed. Old books say the garden was built around 600 B.C. It was located on the bank of the Euphrates River. Today, this area is near Baghdad, Iraq. These gardens were built by a king for his wife. Living in the desert, she missed the plants at her old home. The king wanted to make his queen like their new home more. It may never be known if the Hanging Gardens of Babylon truly existed, but the descriptions of this beautiful place have made their place in history.

_____

_____

_____

_____

_____

_____

_____

Language Arts

2. Organize the following topics into an outline:

Plants
Flowering plants
Mammals
Birds
Sunflowers
Bear
Tulips
Animals
Rhino
Fern
Crow
Nonflowering plants
Algae
Flamingo

I. _____

  A. _____

    i. _____

    ii. _____

  B. _____

    i. _____

    ii. _____

II. _____

  A. _____

    i. _____

    ii. _____

  B. _____

    i. _____

    ii. _____

3. How are the audiences for a research report and a friendly letter different?

Audiences for a research report expect	Audiences for a friendly letter expect

4. **Reorganize these sentences into a paragraph.**

This is a natural way for the earth to release stress.

Let's look at what causes this unpredictable phenomenon.

They can be felt over large geographical areas for brief moments of time.

Did you know that more than a million earthquakes shock the world each year?

Earthquakes are the sudden shock of the earth's surface that result in the earth shaking and rolling.

Language
Arts

5. You would find what kind of information in an atlas?

a. words and their meanings

b. maps or charts

c. groups of synonyms

d. general information

6. The quickest way to search for something on the Internet is to:

9. "Feeble" means

7. Good sources for a research paper include:

a. nonfiction books, library databases, magazines, encyclopedias

b. fiction books, library databases, magazines, encyclopedias

c. nonfiction books, the dictionary, magazines, encyclopedias

d. nonfiction books, library databases, any Internet site, encyclopedias

10. In the dictionary page to the right, is "retain"

a. a noun

b. verb

c. adjective

d. adverb

re·tain / rēˈtān / verb

verb: retain; 3rd person present: retains; past tense: retained; past participle: retained; gerund or present participle: retaining

1. continue to have (something); keep possession of.
"built in 1830, the house retains many of its original features"

• not abolish, discard, or alter.
"the rights of defendants must be retained"

• keep in one's memory.
"I retained a few French words and phrases"

• absorb and continue to hold (a substance).
"limestone is known to retain water"

• keep (something) in place; hold fixed.
"remove the retaining bar"

• keep (someone) engaged in one's service.
"he has been retained as a freelance"

• secure th...

8. What is a bibliography?

a. a list of the books referred to

b. titles of the parts of a book

c. an alphabetical list of names, subjects, etc.,

d. an alphabetical list of terms or words

11. Put a box around the prefix, underline the base word, and circle the suffix of the following word:

unbelievable

12. According to the glossary sample, mass is

> **Marine Organism** organisms that live in the ocean
>
> **Mass** the amount of matter an object has
>
> **Mechanical Energy** the energy of an object or system due to its motion or position

13. Match the parts of speech with their examples:

ran	noun
horse	pronoun
tall	verb
but	adverb
oh	adjective
quickly	conjunction
he	interjection

14. Correct the following run-on sentence.
I love to read books I would read them all day if I could.

_____

_____

_____

_____

15. Circle the sets of pronouns and antecedents that agree.

Sally / he

Timmy / he

house / it

Jake and Timmy / we

Sally and I / us

16. Place the commas and colons in the following sentence.

I have to buy four things at the store milk eggs butter and bread.

Language Arts

17. In theatre, a tragedy is:

a. a play intended to make an audience laugh

b. a play of stories of mysterious adventures

c. a play dealing with tragic events and having an unhappy ending

---

18. Match the literary terms with their examples:

a. bang, biff, clang

b. rubber baby buggy bumpers

c. as hungry as a horse

d. the store was a madhouse

alliteration

onomatopoeia

metaphor

simile

---

19. Plays are divided into:

a. acts

b. chapters

c. sections

---

20. Read this selection.

Mr. and Mrs. Brown first met Paddington on a railway platform. In fact, that was how he came to have such an unusual name for a bear, for Paddington was the name of the station.

The Browns were there to meet their daughter Judy, who was coming home from school for the holidays. It was a warm summer day and the station was crowded with people on their way to the seaside.

Trains were humming, loudspeakers blaring, porters rushing about shouting at one another, and altogether there was so much noise that Mr Brown, who saw him first, had to tell his wife several times before she understood.

"A bear? On Paddington station?" Mrs Brown looked at her husband in amazement. "Don't be silly, Henry. There can't be!"

Mr Brown adjusted his glasses. "But there is," he insisted. "I distinctly saw it. Over there – near the bicycle rack. It was wearing a funny kind of hat."

On a scale of 1 to 10, how much did you enjoy it?

History
& Geography

1. Check the landmark that the Inca built.

 A.

 B.

 C.

2. List reasons explorers set out to explore:

3. The Medici family is known for:

4. Henry VIII was king of:

5. Draw a line to match the climate zones with their characteristics

 A.

 B.

 C.

Tropical   Polar   Temperate

History
& Geography

⑤ ① ② ⑥ ④ ③

Lakes

Caspian Sea

Lake Michigan

Lake Victoria

Mountains

Mt. Fuji

Mt. Everest

Denali

6. Using the map above, name the lakes marked in orange.

1. _____

2. _____

3. _____

7. Using the map above, name the mountains marked in green.

4. _____

5. _____

6. _____

8. Using the map above, color the country and label with the corresponding number.

1. Canada   3. India   5. Australia

2. France   4. Egypt   6. Brazil

9. Daniel Boone is famous for:

10. Circle the events that led to the American Civil War.

Harper's Ferry Raid

Taxation without Representation

Lincoln Elected President

The Assassination of Archduke Ferdinand

South Carolina Secedes

The Sinking of The Maine

Missouri Compromise

The Attack on the Alamo

Dred Scott Decision

The Bombing of the World Trade Center

11. Manifest Destiny refers to:

a. a set of proposals put forward by U.S. President Harry S. Truman to Congress in his January 1949 State of the Union address

b. the 19th-century doctrine or belief that the expansion of the US throughout the American continents was both justified and inevitable.

c. a principle of US policy, originated by President James Monroe in 1823, that any intervention by external powers in the politics of the Americas is a potentially hostile act against the US.

12. The Transcontinental Railroad was completed in

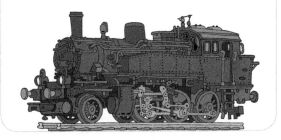

13. Match the states with their climates.

Arizona	swamp
California	mountains
Colorado	prairie
Kansas	green rolling hills
Louisiana	mountains by the sea
Missouri	desert

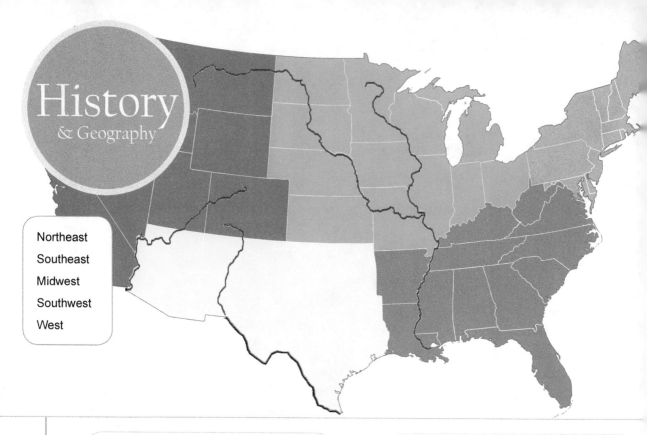

Northeast
Southeast
Midwest
Southwest
West

14. Label the regions of the United States by color:

Orange:
_____

Blue:
_____

Green:
_____

Yellow:
_____

Red:
_____

15. Draw a line to match the states with their capitals.

Missouri	Jefferson City
Nebraska	Carson City
Oregon	Lincoln
Maine	Augusta
Nevada	Salem

16. Using the map above, can you point to where the following rivers are in the United States.

Colorado River   Rio Grande River

Missouri River   Mississippi River

17. Match the art with its country

A. Australia

B. United States

C. Egypt

D. China

E. Russia

Silk Painting

Totem Pole

Painted Egg

Cave Painting

Pectoral

18. Match the instrument with its location

A. Scotland

B. Caribbean

C. Australia

D. Poland

E. Japan

F. North America

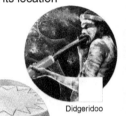
Didgeridoo

Drum

Gong

Accordion

Steel Drums

Bagpipes

19. *let's celebrate!*

Match the holiday with the country

Israel	St. Lucia's Day
China	St. Patrick's Day
Sweden	Cinco de Mayo
Iran	Dragon Boat Festival
Ireland	Passover
Mexico	Ramadan

20. Circle the world foods that you have eaten.

Sushi   Spaghetti   Naan   Tacos   Fried Rice   Pita   Falafel

Science

1. Circle the characteristics of vertebrates

Have a spine   Have an internal skeleton

Do not have a spine   Have an external skeleton

2. Circle the five kingdoms of living things.

Plants   Corn

Bacteria   Eukaryotes

Animals   Fish

Yeast   Fungi

Prokaryotes   Mold

3. Single-celled organisms include:

4. Label the parts of the cell.

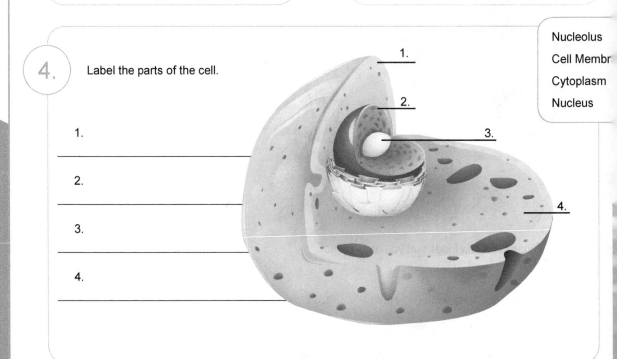

Nucleolus
Cell Membr
Cytoplasm
Nucleus

1.

_____

2.

_____

3.

_____

4.

_____

5. Label the parts of the respiratory system.

1. _____

2. _____

3. _____

4. _____

5. _____

1. ─────
2. ─────
3. ─────
4. ─────
5. ─────

Larynx

Lung

Trachea

Nasal Cavity

Bronchus

Oral Cavity

6.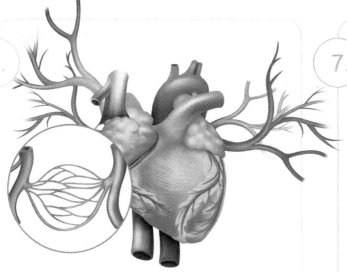

Organs of the circulatory system include:

7. The endocrine system helps your body by

8. Smoking and alcohol abuse can cause

9. A nonvascular plant is

a. a plant that is characterized by the presence of conducting tissue

b. a plant that is characterized by the presence of no conducting tissue

10. Label the parts of the flower

Sepal
Petal
Stamen
Pistil

1.

2.

3.

4.

11. Photosynthesis is

12. Match the plant with the way it reproduces.

_____ ASEXUAL

_____ SPORE-BEARING

_____ NON-FLOWERING SEED

_____ FLOWERING

A. Any type of vascular plant that reproduces via an exposed seed

B. A plant that produces flowers

C. Roots such as corms, stem tubers, rhizomes, and stolon undergo vegetative reproduction.

D. Produces a unit of sexual or asexual reproduction that may be adapted for dispersal and for survival

13. Bacteria reproduce by

- **a.** Giving birth
- **b.** Laying eggs
- **c.** Finding a host
- **d.** Binary fission

14. Match the animal with the way it reproduces

| Cow | Robin | Starfish | Shark | Earthworm |

Egg

Eggs and Regeneration

Eggs hatch in mother and are birthed

Live Young

Eggs and Regeneration

15. Animals that are able to regenerate include:

16. Put the growth stages in order

Science

17. Examples of elements include:

18. Label the parts of the atom

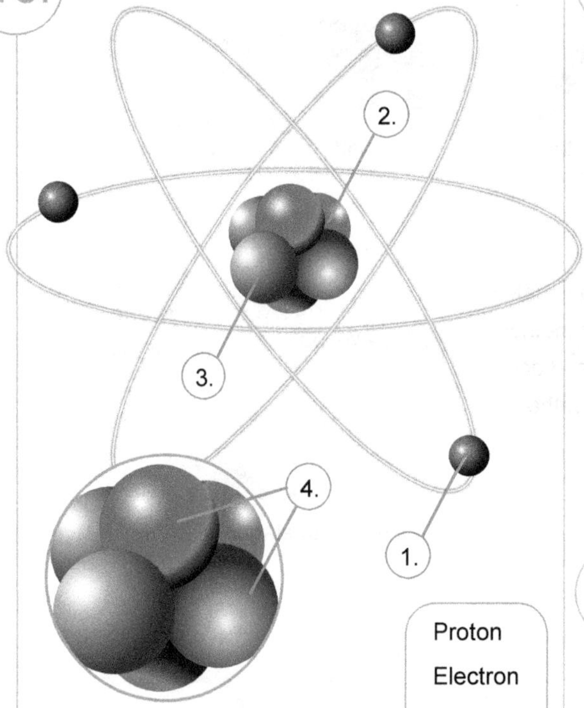

Proton
Electron
Nucleus
Neutron

1. _____

2. _____

3. _____

4. _____

19. Circle the examples of physical changes.

Crushing

Cooking

Melting

Electroplating

Boiling

Rotting

Mixing

20. Circle the examples of chemical changes.

Breaking

Rusting

Shredding

Burning

Chopping

Digestion

Bible

1. Match the prophet with his work or message.

Isaiah   Confronted David about his sin

Jeremiah   Calls Israel to repent and rebuild the temple

Ezekiel   Saw a vision of dry bones being made alive

Daniel   Was also a priest

Jonah   Was sent to Nineveh

Obadiah   Prophesied about the Messiah

Haggai   Was a prophet in Babylon

Samuel   Anointed Israel's first king

Nathan   Preached about God's justice

2. Put the events of Joseph's life in order.

_____ Became a ruler in Egypt

_____ Sold as a slave

_____ Given a coat of many colors

_____ Reunited with his brothers

_____ Made friends with a baker

_____ Thrown into a pit

_____ Worked for Potipher

_____ Interpreted Pharoah's dream

_____ Became a Father

_____ Sent to prison

3. Match the event of Jesus' ministry with the description.

1. Jesus turned water into wine

2. Jesus caused the blind to see

3. Jesus appeared to His disciples

4. Jesus resurrected the dead

5. Jesus healed someone of bleeding

☐ Road to Emmaus

☐ Mary and Martha's Home

☐ Healing of Bartemaus

☐ Journey to Jairus' House

☐ Wedding at Cana

4. Esther was

Bible

5. A concordance is used for

6. Circle the uses of a Bible dictionary.

See pictures of Bible objects

Learn Greek words

Learn about customs in Bible times

Learn Hebrew words

Learn definitions of words

Find verses about a topic

7. Look up these passages:

Proverbs 12:1

Galatians 3:22

Joshua 24:14

8. Find these locations on the map below.

Egypt	Ur of Chaldea
Euphrates River	Tigris River
Mt. Ararat	Babylon

Noah's Ark

Mt. Ararat
Noah's Ark 2452 BC

Tigris

Haran
(Sultantepe)

Euphrates

Babylon founded 2300 BC

Bethel
Hebron
Shechem
Ai

Egypt

Euphrates

Tigris

River of Egypt

En Mishpat
(Kadesh Barnea
Gen 14:7; El Beidha)

Ur of Chaldea
(Tell Muqqayyar)
Tower of Babel 2275 BC

Tower of Babel

Pyramids
2200 BC

Egypt

34

9. Fill in the blanks for Eph. 4:29.

Do not let any _____ talk come out of your mouths, but only

what is _____ for _____ others up according to

their _____, that it may _____ those who listen.

10. Fill in the blanks for Psalm 1

_____ is the one who does not _____ in step with the wicked

or _____ in the way that sinners take or _____ in the company of

mockers, but whose delight is in the _____ of the Lord, and who meditates on

his law day and _____.

11. Put these verses of the Romans Road in order.

_____ Romans 3:23

_____ Romans 5:8

_____ Romans 10:13

_____ Romans 6:23

_____ Romans 10:9-10

_____ Romans 10:23

12. Fill in the blanks for John 1:9-10

9 If we _____ our sins, he is

faithful and just and will _____

us our sins and purify us from all

_____.

10 If we claim we have not sinned, we

make him out to be a _____ and

his _____ is not in us.

13. Atonement means

☐   **a.** the action or process of forgiving or being forgiven

  b. the reconciliation of God and humankind through Jesus Christ

  c. sincere regret or remorse

14. Circle the examples of repentance.

Saying mean things   Insisting on my own way

Obeying parents   Looking out for others

Saying kind things   Disobeying parents

15. A covenant is

a. a declaration or assurance that one will do a particular thing or that a particular thing will happen

b. the reconciliation of God and human-kind through Jesus Christ

c. an agreement between two or more persons

18. George Whitefield was known for

16. Redemption is

a. the action of saving or being saved from sin, error, or evil

b. the action or process of forgiving or being forgiven

c. a declaration or assurance that one will do a particular thing or that a particular thing will happen declaration or assurance that one will do a particular thing or that a particular thing will happen

19. William Carey was a missionary to

17. George Müller was known for

20. Amy Carmichael was known for

STUDENT PLACEMENT TEST ADMINISTRATOR GUIDE

In the following pages, you will find the student placement test administrator guide. This section walks you through assessing your child during the test and includes an answer key and scoring chart.

SECTIONS

Each subject test is divided into 5 sections. This allows you to break up the test as needed and evaluate based on both individual section scores and an overall subject score.

ASSESS

This column includes questions and information to help you understand the goal of the test question. Use these questions to help identify and assess knowledge of the subject matter or understanding of processes, whether or not your child answers correctly.

ANSWERS

This column indicates the correct answer for the questions. Occasionally this column is merged with the notes column to give ample room for detailed answer information.

NOTES

In order to help you understand how a child should arrive at an answer, we have included this section to give the details of the processes. As well, this area includes helpful tips on the goals for the question and how your child should arrive at answers.

✓ SCORES

Use this area to indicate a correct answer or sufficient knowledge to give credit for the question. Use either a checkmark or a number one. As your child completes each section, add up the marks and place the total in the "Section Score" box at the top of the section. These scores will be used to tally your child's subject and overall scores at the end of the test.

SUMMARY

The final page of this section is used to summarize the section scores, subject scores, and overall grade placement.

TEST HACKS

Combat test nervousness and reduce stress by utilizing some of these Test Hacks.

1. Prepare snacks in advance, including protein to munch on during the test and other snacks for break time.

2. When choosing a test location, consider where your child learns best, even if that means lounging in a hammock or sitting on an exercise ball.

3. Grab a stress ball, Silly Putty, gum, or other little tools to have on hand to combat fidgetiness.

4. If your child seems nervous, add in a little fun by periodically surprising them with a question like, "What is your favorite color?" or asking them to do something funny like draw a goofy alien with horns.

5. If you begin seeing signs of stress during the test, take a break to do jumping jacks, take 10 deep breaths, or go for a 15-minute walk or bike ride.

6. Diffusing a citrus oil like lemon, grapefruit, or orange is good to alleviate stress and improve focus without using overly calming scents like lavender.

PLACEMENT TEST GUIDE

Use when administering and scoring

STUDENT PLACEMENT TEST GUIDE

#	Assess	Answer	Notes	✔
WHOLE NUMBERS TO THE BILLIONS			Section Score	
1	Is your child able to understand numbers without using objects? Does your child place commas within the number?	1,129,201,016		
2	Does your child know that a prime number is only divisible by itself and 1?	17 and 43	The first few prime numbers are 2, 3, 5, 7, 11, 13, 17, 19, 23, and 29.	
3	Does your child know that a factor is a number that will go into another number?	9	Find all the numbers that will divide into each number. The largest number that will divide into both is the greatest common factor.	
4	Does your child know that a common multiple is a number that both numbers will go into?	12	Begin multiplying by 1, 2, 3,.... The lowest number that both number multiply into is the least common multiple.	
RATIOS AND PERCENTS			Section Score	
5	Does your child write answers in the correct units? Does your child write the ratio and then reduce it to lowest terms?	3:4	Compare girls: boys, which is 18:24. Reduce that to lowest terms by dividing by 6.	
6	Does your child calculate how many inches each side will be before drawing?	6 in. x 10 in.	Use graph paper to keep lines straight. The shorter side is 12 ft., so divide that by 2 to get the scale of 6 in. The longer side is 20 ft., so divide that by 2 to get the scale of 10 in.	
7	Does your child multiply 75 by 55%? Does he or she round?	41	Multiply 75 by 0.55. This gives you 41.25. Round to the nearest whole number, so round down to 41.	
8	Does your child understand that decimals, fractions, and percents are basically the same things written different ways?	0.96 and $^{24}/_{25}$	96% is 96 hundredths, which give 0.96. The fraction is 96/100. Reduce to lowest terms by dividing by 4 to get 24/25.	
FRACTIONS AND DECIMALS			Section Score	
9	Does your child keep work neat? Sloppiness leads to errors. Does your child understand that fractions must have the same denominator to be compared?	12	Find the least common multiple by multiplying each denominator by 1, 2, 3,....The lowest number that both 4 and 6 multiply to is the lowest common denominator.	
10	Does your child understand that fractions are reduced by dividing the numerator and denominator by the same number?	$^4/_7$	Divide the numerator and the denominator by 5.	

#	Assess	Answer	Notes	✓
FRACTIONS AND DECIMALS CONT.				
11	Does your child write out the problem and then shift the decimal? Does he or she add zeros as place holders?	0.013	Since 300 is a 3-digit number, add a zero to the end of 3.9. Bring the decimal up to the quotient and add a zero over the 9 as a place holder. Continue to divide, adding zeros until it divides evenly.	
12	Does your child know the tenths place? Does he or she know how to round?	11.3	The tenth's place is one place to the right of the decimal. Round the 2 up.	
MULTIPLICATION AND DIVISION			Section Score	
13	Does your child show signs of estimating what a correct answer would be and rechecking answers? Does your child line up the columns and carry?	38,469,561	Multiply the ones. Shift down and over and multiply the tens. Shift down and over and multiply the hundreds. Shift down and over and multiply the thousands. Add the products together and write commas.	
14	Does your child line up the quotient with the dividend? Does he or she bring numbers down?	261	Divide 312 into 814. Multiply by 312 and subtract. Bring down the 3. Divide, multiply, and subtract. Bring down the 2. Divide, multiply, and subtract.	
15	Does your child eliminate possible answers immediately?	1,000	4,832 rounded to the nearest thousand is 5,000. 5,000 divided by 5 is 1,000.	
16	Does your child write a division problem?	6	Multiply 12 doughnuts in a dozen by 3 dozen. This is 36. Add the parents to the children. This is 6. Divide 36 by 6.	
GEOMETRY			Section Score	
17	Does your child understand that variables in formulas represent actual numbers? Does your child know how to use a ruler and protractor?		Draw a 1 in. line. Place the center of the protractor on the end of the line and align the line on the protractor with the line you have drawn. Being sure to use the correct set of numbers, make a tick next to 35. Remove the protractor and lay the ruler between the tick mark and the end you place the protractor on. Draw a 3 in. line coming from the 1 in. line.	
18	Does your child use the correct formula?	64 sq. ft.	Use the formula Area=A+B/2 x H. A is the top line. B is the base. H is the height. A(6) + B(10) = 16. 16 divided by 2 is 8. 8 x H (8) = 64.	
19	Does your child divide the shape into simpler shapes before attempting to solve?	Volume = 120 cu. ft. Surface area = 148 sq. ft.	Use the volume formula Area = lwh. L is length, w is width, h is height. Area = 6x5x4 = 120. Use the surface area formula Area = 2wl + 2lh + 2hw. W is width, l is length, and h is height. 2x5x6 + 2x6x4 + 2x5x4 = 60+48+40 = 148 sq. ft.	
20	Does your child know to compare the sides and angles of triangles? equilateral Isosceles right-angle scalene acute obtuse		• A right-angle triangle is a triangle in which one angle is a right angle (that is, a 90° angle). • An acute triangle is a triangle with all three angles acute (less than 90°). • An obtuse triangle is one with one obtuse angle (greater than 90°) and two acute angles. • A scalene triangle is a triangle that has three unequal sides. • An isosceles triangle is a triangle that has two sides of equal length. • An equilateral triangle is a triangle in which all three sides are equal.	

STUDENT PLACEMENT TEST GUIDE

#	Assess	Answer	Notes	✔
WRITING			Section Score	
1	Is the summary shorter than the original, and does your child use his or her own words?		The summary should be written in complete sentences with proper punctuation and capitalization. It should be in the child's own words and include almost all of the following words: Greeks, Great Pyramid, Giza, Egypt, Hanging Gardens of Babylon, Euphrates River.	
2	Does your child recognize that some points are more important than others?		I. Plants A. Flowering Plants i. Sunflowers ii. Tulips B. Nonflowering Plants i. Fern ii. Algae II. Animals A. Mammals i. Bear ii. Rhino B. Birds i. Crow ii. Flamingo The I/II, A/B, and i/ii levels may be in different orders, but they must be in the same levels of the outline.	
3	Does your child recognize that there are different levels of formality and different types of information in pieces of literature?		Acceptable answers include: Audiences for a research report expect facts, numbers, interesting information, and formal writing. Audiences for a friendly letter expect fun stories, personal thoughts, questions, and informal writing.	
4	Does your child understand that paragraphs contain topic, supporting, and concluding sentences?		Answer: Earthquakes are the sudden shock of the earth's surface that result in the earth shaking and rolling. They can be felt over large geographical areas for brief moments of time. This is a natural way for the earth to release stress. Did you know that more than a million earthquakes shock the world each year? This first sentence states that the paragraph is about earthquakes. "They" in the second sentence refers back to earthquakes and describes them. "This" in the third sentence refers back to earthquakes and explains why they happen. The last sentence leaves the reader with a thought.	

#	Assess	Answer	Notes	✔
RESEARCH			Section Score	
5	Is your child familiar with different reference resources whether or not he or she has used them?	B.	An atlas contains maps and information such as climate and population for specific areas.	
6	Is your child able to use the Internet in a supervised way?	Acceptable answers include: get a parent, use a search engine, visit a trusted site, use a library database, etc.		
7	Does your child know where to find different types of information? Does he or she know the difference between reliable sources and unreliable sources?	A.	Fiction books are primarily made up. The dictionary does not give enough information. Some Internet sites are not written by experts.	
8	Does your child understand that he or she should give credit to sources? Does he or she know that most citations require author, title, and date?	A.	A bibliography is included in formal research papers and in many nonfiction books. It gives credit to other sources and shows that the author has researched the subject thoroughly.	
SPELLING AND VOCABULARY			Section Score	
9	Does your child read and think about each definition? Does he or she put the word in a sentence?	Acceptable answers include: frail, weak, fragile, week, puny, sickly, tamed, etc.		
10	Does your child understand how to read a dictionary entry?	B. Verb.	The child should first find the word and then read the entry to find the part of speech.	
11	Does your child show an understanding of prefixes, base words, and suffixes?	"Un-" is the prefix because it comes before the word. "Believ" is the base word because it gives the idea. "-able" is the suffix because it comes at the end of the word.		
12	Does your child show evidence of searching for the word alphabetically?	The amount of matter an object contains.	The child should find the word and copy the definition. The goal of this question is to see if your child is able to use a glossary well. If you would like to test further, use a book from your own library.	
GRAMMAR AND USAGE			Section Score	
13	Does your child know the basic definition and some examples of the parts of speech?	horse / noun he / pronoun ran / verb qickly / adverb tall / adjective but / conjunction oh / interjection	A noun is a person, place, thing, or idea. A pronoun refers to a noun. A verb shows action or a state of being. An adverb modifies a verb, adjective, or other adverb. An adjective modifies a noun. A conjunction joins thoughts or ideas. An interjection is an abrupt remark.	

#	Assess	Answer	Notes	✔
14	Does your child understand what a run-on sentence is and the different ways it can be corrected?	I love to read books; I would read them all day if I could. I love to read books, and I would read them all day if I could. I love to read books. I would read them all day if I could. Because I love to read books, I would read them all day if I could. A run-on can be corrected by adding a colon, adding a comma and a conjunction, separating it into two sentences, or making one sentence subordinate to another.		
15	Does your child understand what pronouns and antecedents are?	Timmy / he house / it Sally and I / us	Pronouns must match the word they refer to in number and gender.	
16	Does your child know the difference between commas and colons?	I have to buy four things at the store: milk, eggs, butter, and bread. The colon comes before the list. The commas separate the items in the list.		
LITERATURE			Section Score	
17	Does your child know basic theatrical terms?	C.	Other plays include comedies and romances.	
18	Is your child able to comprehend the examples? Is he or she familiar with these literary terms?	alliteration - rubber baby buggy bumpers (Alliteration uses the same letter or sound at the beginning of several words.) onomatopoeia - bang, biff, clang (Onomatopoeia is a word that sounds like a noise.) metaphor - the store was a madhouse (A metaphor brings an image to mind.) simile - as hungry as a horse (A simile makes a comparison.)		
19	Does your child know what acts and scenes are?	A.	Books are divided into chapter. Sections is a very general term.	
20	Did your child enjoy the selection? If not, was it because reading and comprehension is a struggle or because the selection was not interesting?	There is no right or wrong answer. This is for you to measure how much the child enjoys reading and he or she likes to read.		

Notes

STUDENT PLACEMENT TEST GUIDE

#	Assess	Answer	Notes	✓
WORLD HISTORY			Section Score	
1	Is your child familiar with the Inca? Does he or she recognize any of the other landmarks?	C.	A - Great Wall of China B - Parthenon in Greece C - Inca Pyramid	
2	Does your child understand that explorers were looking for wealth, fame, or trade routes? Does he or she understand that political leaders funded exploration to gain power?	Acceptable answers include: to learn more, to gain territory, to find riches, to open trade routes, to spread religion		
3	Is your child familiar with the Renaissance? Has he or she heard of the Medici?	Acceptable answers include: ruling Florence, supporting the arts, inventing modern banking, promoting the Renaissance, etc.		
4	Does your child know other English monarchs?	England.		
WORLD GEOGRAPHY			Section Score	
5	Does your child understand that climate changes with different areas of the world?	Polar - C. Temperate - A. Tropical - B.		
6	Does your child know what a lake is?	1. Lake Michigan 2. Caspian Sea 3. Lake Victoria		
7	Does your child understand what a mountain is?	4.Mt. Everest 5.Denali 6. Mt. Fuji		
8	Is your child able to at least get the correct continent when locating countries?	Answers on map on page 44.		
UNITED STATES HISTORY			Section Score	
9	Has your child heard of Daniel Boone?	Acceptable answers include: his skill as a woodsman, opening the wilderness trail, settling Kentucky, moving to Missouri, being captured by the Shawnee.		
10	Does your child understand that there were several causes for the Civil War? Does he or she understand that each region views the causes differently?	Harper's Ferry Raid Lincoln Elected President South Carolina Secedes Missouri Compromise Dred Scott Decision		

1. Canada
2. France
3. India
4. Egypt
5. Australia
6. Brazil

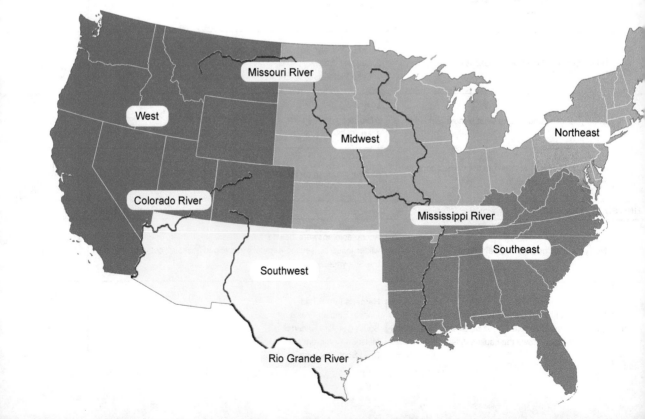

Missouri River

West

Midwest

Northeast

Colorado River

Mississippi River

Southeast

Southwest

Rio Grande River

STUDENT PLACEMENT TEST GUIDE

#	Assess	Answer	Notes	✓
11.	Does your child understand why America began expanding West?	B.		
12.	Does your child have an idea of the time period of the railroad? Does he or she understand the benefits of completing the Transcontinental Railroad?	D.	If your child does not know the exact date, does he or she understand that it was completed after the Civil War in the later part of the 1800s?	

UNITED STATES GEOGRAPHY · Section Score

#	Assess	Answer	Notes	✓
13.	Does your child have a general knowledge of the climate of different parts of the United States?	California - mountains by the sea Arizona - desert Colorado - mountains Kansas - prairie Missouri - green rolling hills Louisiana - swamp		
14.	Does your child understand that ways of life are different across the United States?	Reference Map to the Left. Orange - Northeast Blue - Southeast Green - Midwest Yellow - Southwest Red - West		
15.	Does your child know some of the states and capitals?	Missouri - Jefferson City Nebraska - Omaha Oregon - Salem Maine - Augusta Nevada - Carson City		
16.	Is your child able to label the Mississippi and Missouri rivers correctly?	Reference Map to the Left. • The Colorado River is goes from Colorado to the border between California and Arizona. • The Missouri River goes from Montana to Missouri. • The Rio Grande follows the border between Texas and Mexico. • The Mississippi goes along the borders of Iowa, Illinois, Missouri, Kentucky, Tennessee, Arkansas, Mississippi, and Louisiana		

CULTURE		Section Score
17.	Does your child enjoy looking at art from different times and places?	A. Australia - cave paintings B. U.S. - Totem Pole C. Egypt - pectoral D. China - silk painting E. Russia - painted egg	
18.	Does your child enjoy music from different times and places?	Didgeridoo - Australia Gong - Japan Accordion - Poland Bagpipes - Scotland Steel Drums - Caribbean Drum - North America	
19.	Does your child take an interest in different holidays?	St. Lucia's Day - Sweden St. Patrick's Day - Ireland Cinco de Mayo - Mexico Dragon Boat Festival - China Passover - Israel Ramadan - Iran	
20.	Is your child willing to try new foods from around the world?	If your child has not had any of these foods, talk about regional or international foods he or she has eaten.	

Notes

STUDENT PLACEMENT TEST GUIDE

#	Assess	Answer	Notes	✓
LIVING THINGS			Section Score	
1	Does your child understand that some animals internal skeletons and some do not?	Vertebrates have a spine and an internal skeleton.		
2	Does your child understand that there are plants, animals, two types of single-celled organisms, and fungi?	Plants, Animals, Prokaryotes, Eukaryotes, Fungi. The other items are examples from each kingdom.		
3	Does your child know what a single-celled organism is?	Answers may include: bacteria, viruses, protozoans, algae, amoeba, etc.		
4	Does your child understand that cells have different parts that have different jobs?	1. Cell membrane 2. Nucleus 3. Nucleolus 4. Cytoplasm		
HUMAN BODY			Section Score	
5	Does your child know that the lungs bring in oxygen and get rid of carbon dioxide?	1. Nasal Cavity 2. Oral Cavity 3. Larynx 4. Trachea 5. Bronchus 6. Lung		
6	Does your child know that the circulatory system transports blood and that the blood carries oxygen and nutrients?	Answers may include: heart, arteries, capillaries, veins, or blood.		
7	Does your child understand that hormones regulate how your body works?	Answers may include: produce hormones, regulate cells or organs, regulate the body's growth, regulate metabolism, etc.		
8	Is your child aware that choices we make affect our health?	Answers may include lung disease, cancer, asthma, heart disease, high blood pressure, emotional changes, insomnia, depression, liver damage, weak immune system.		
PLANTS			Section Score	
9	Does your child know that not all plants are the same?	B.	Nonvascular plants include mosses, liverworts, and hornworts	
10	Does your child understand that flowers must be pollinated to produce fruit?	1. Petal 2. Pistil (some texts may use carpel instead of pistil) 3. Stamen 4. Sepal		

#	Assess	Answer	Notes	✓
11	Is your child aware that plants make their own food?	Acceptable answers include: Photo means "light" and synthesis means "putting together," the process through which plants use water and carbon dioxide to create their food, or how plants make their own food.		
12	Does your child know that not all plants reproduce in the same way?	Asexual - Roots such as corms, stem tubers, rhizomes, and stolon undergo vegetative reproduction. Spore-bearing - Produces a unit of sexual or asexual reproduction that may be adapted for dispersal and for survival Nonflowering seed - any type of vascular plant that reproduce via an exposed seed Flowering seed - a plant that produces flowers		
LIFE CYCLES			Section Score	
13	Does your child understand that single-celled organisms do not reproduce through eggs or live birth?	D.		
14	Does your child understand that animals reproduce differently?	Cow - live young Earthworm - eggs and regeneration Robin - Egg Starfish - Eggs and regeneration Shark - eggs hatch in mother and are birthed		
15	Is your child aware that some animals can regrow body parts?	Acceptable answers include: lizards, flat worms, sea cucumbers, sharks, spiders, sponges, starfish, earthworms		
16	Does your child know that there are different stages growth and development in living things?	infancy, childhood, adolescence, adulthood		
CHEMISTRY			Section Score	
17	Does your child understand that substances can be broken down to elements or combinations of elements.	Acceptable answers include: oxygen, hydrogen, sodium, chlorine, lead, iron. Elements are substances that cannot be chemically interconverted or broken down into simpler substances and are primary constituents of matter.		
18	Does your child know that matter is made of atoms?	1. Electron 3. Neutron 2. Proton 4. Nucleus		
19	Is your child aware that objects can be changed physically but are still made up of the same thing?	Crushing Boiling Melting Mixing		
20	Does your child understand that substances can be combined in ways to make new substances?	Rusting Burning Digesting		

STUDENT PLACEMENT TEST GUIDE

#	Assess	Answer	Notes	✔
IBLE STORIES			Section Score	
1	Does your child understand that prophets called God's people to repentance and pointed forward to Christ?	Isaiah - prophesied about the Messiah Jeremiah - was also a priest Ezekiel - saw a vision of dry bones being made alive Daniel - was a prophet in Babylon Jonah - was sent to Nineveh Obadiah - preached about God's justice Haggai - called Israel to repent and rebuild the temple Samuel - anointed Israel's first king Nathan - confronted David about his sin		
2	Is your child aware that Joseph was a son of Jacob?	1. Given a coat of many colors 2. Thrown into a pit 3. Sold as a slave 4. Worked for Potipher 5. Sent to prison 6. Made friends with a baker 7. Interpreted Pharoah's dream 8. Became a ruler in Egypt 9. Became a Father 10. Reunited with his brothers		
3	Does your child understand the significance of Jesus' signs and wonders?	Road to Emmaus - 3. Jesus appeared to His disciples Mary and Martha's Home - 4. Jesus resurrected the dead Healing of Bartemaus - 2. Jesus caused the blind to see Journey to Jairus' House - 5. healed someone of bleeding Wedding at Cana - 1. Jesus turned water into wine		
4	Does your child understand that God uses people to accomplish His will?	Acceptable answers include: a Jew, the wife of Ahasuerus, the one who saved her people, Mordecai's niece, a queen		
BIBLE REFERENCE TOOLS			Section Score	
5	Does your child understand that a concordance can help him or her find a particular passage?	Acceptable answers include: finding verses about a topic, learning Greek words, learning Hebrew words, getting meanings of specific words in the Bible		
6	Does your child know that he or she can use a Bible dictionary to look up words he or she does not understand?	See pictures of Bible objects Learn about customs in Bible times Learn definitions of words		
7	Is your child able to find all passages quickly without using the Table of Contents or singing a song?	This is a subjective question. Just watch to see that your child goes to the correct testament, book, chapter, then verse without using the table of contents.		

STUDENT PLACEMENT TEST GUIDE

#	Assess	Answer	Notes	✓
8	Does your child understand that the places in the Bible really existed?			
BIBLE PASSAGES			Section Score	
9	Does your child know that he or she should guard his or her words?	unwholesome; helpful; building; needs; benefit		
10	Does your child understand the difference between a righteous man and a wicked man?	Blessed; walk; stand; sit; law; night		
11	Can your child explain the way of salvation?	Romans 3:23 Romans 6:23 Romans 5:8 Romans 10:9-10 Romans 10:13 Romans 10:23		
12	Does your child understand that Jesus is the light and that we are to walk in the light?	confess; forgive; unrighteousness; liar; word		
THEOLOGY			Section Score	
13	Does your child understand that a perfect blood sacrifice was needed for sin and that all sacrifices in the Old Testament pointed to Christ?	B.		
14	Does your child know that repentance involves ceasing to do wrong and beginning to do right?	Obeying parents Saying kind things Looking out for others		
15	Can your child explain that a covenant is an agreement between two or more persons?	C.		
16	Does your child understand that believers are bought with the blood of Christ?	A.		
CHURCH HISTORY AND MISSIONS			Section Score	
17	Is your child familiar with the names of missionaries?	Acceptable answers include: his work with orphans, his belief that he should not trust in a bank account, his prayer life, his wild youth		
18	Does your child take an interest in other countries and cultures?	Acceptable answers include: his sermons, the Great Awakening, his booming voice		
19	Does your child desire to meet the needs of others?	India		
20		Acceptable answers include: her work with young girls, her work in India, her brown eyes, her disguises		

MATH

Score	Section		Total Score
	Whole Numbers to the Billions		
	Ratio and Percents		
	Fractions and Decimals		Grade Placement
	Multiplication and Division		
	Geometry		

LANGUAGE ARTS

Score	Section		Total Score
	Writing		
	Research		
	Spelling & Vocabulary		Grade Placement
	Grammar & Usage		
	Literature		

HISTORY & GEOGRAPHY

Score	Section		Total Score
	World History		
	World Geography		
	United States History		Grade Placement
	United States Geography		
	Culture		

SCIENCE

Score	Section		Total Score
	Living Things		
	Human Body		
	Plants		Grade Placement
	Life Cycles		
	Chemistry		

BIBLE

Score	Section		Total Score
	Bible Stories		
	Bible Reference Tools		
	Bible Passages		Grade Placement
	Theology		
	Church History and Missions		

STUDENT PLACEMENT SCORING

The Well Planned Start was designed to assess a grade level *per subject.* Use the key below to *determine the grade level for each subject.*

1. Each correct answer is valued at 1 point. Count the number in each section. Write the number in the score box to the left of the section.

2. Add the section scores together and place the total in the **Total Score** box.

3. Using the key below, determine the grade assessment for *each subject.*

SUBJECT TEST KEY

- Total Score = 20: Administer the 6th grade test for this subject. Your child may be ready for 7th grade.
- Total Score = 15-19: Your child is ready for the 6th grade.
- Total Score = 10-14: Base your decision on the following **section scores.**
  - Score 2 or less in 1-2 sections: Your child is ready for the 6th grade in this subject, but you can expect to give extra help throughout the year.
  - Score 2 or less in 3-5 sections: Your child should begin this subject at a 5th grade level.
- All sections = 0-9: Administer the 4th grade test for this subject. Your child needs additional evaluation.

BIBLE EXCEPTION

Because the development of spiritual growth is not confined to a grade level, the Bible tests for Well Planned Start were designed to cover a range through the following stages of education:

- Starting Out - Preschool - 1st Grade
- Getting Exciting: 2nd - 4th Grade
- Beginning to Understand: 5th - 8th Grade
- Learning to Reason: 9th - 12th Grade

When scoring Bible and determining placement, it is recommended to use your discretion in deciding if additional testing is needed or more time studying the topics covered.

WHAT NEXT?

Compare your findings to the parent assessment test and begin to make a plan of action on the following page.

If you suspect a learning challenge or special needs, we strongly recommend additional testing with a specialist.

MATH

grade

_____
_____
_____
_____
_____
_____
_____

LANGUAGE ARTS

grade

_____
_____
_____
_____
_____
_____
_____

HISTORY & GEOGRAPHY

grade

_____
_____
_____
_____
_____
_____
_____

SCIENCE

_____
_____
_____
_____
_____
_____
_____

BIBLE

_____
_____
_____
_____
_____
_____
_____

PLAN OF ACTION

Your child has completed the test, the scores are tallied, and a grade level is determined. But, it doesn't stop there! Here are some ways to utilize the information gleaned from this assessment to help you and your child tackle the new school year with confidence!

HOMESCHOOL

Use this space to note your child's grade level, gaps you observed during testing, areas where your child excels, and specific strategies you will be seeking as you choose curriculum. Make a list of academic needs for the coming year, and have that list on hand to check against the content in your curricula of choice.

HYBRIDS - CO-OP, TUTORIAL, & ENRICHMENTS

If your child is involved in homeschool classes taught through a co-op, use this area to note learning needs to discuss with your child's teacher(s). Also, make note of any enrichment activities you can do with your child to fill in gaps and strengthen weaknesses.

TRADITIONAL SCHOOL

If your child attends a private or public school, make note of areas you want to discuss with your child's teacher(s) to determine how to strengthen weaknesses. At home, plan trips or organize evening discussion to cater to strengths and incorporate Bible training.

BEGINNING TO UNDERSTAND

PARENT TEACHING TIPS

Somewhere around fourth or fifth grade, a tangible change begins to take place in your child. Connections start clicking into place. Light bulbs come on. An understanding dawns. The change is subtle at first, but, as you ask comprehension questions, discuss prayer requests, or explore the impact of experiences, you will notice a new depth to your child's conversational contributions.

These understanding years, typically fitting into what is now referred to as middle school, form a bridge between the years of excitement and the deeper thinking required in high school.

So, what does this look like practically?

1. Do the algebra. Many of you are groaning right now, but algebraic equations are a perfect example of the connections being made during this stage. Children will begin to learn that if A+B=C and D+E=C, then it must follow that A+B=D+E. The connections occur as often in everyday life as they do in math, science, and logic. Learning the dreaded algebraic formulas truly does help growing minds process the connection and balance in other areas.

2. Explore inferences. A paragraph that discusses "steam rising from wet pavement as the clouds parted, allowing the hot summer sun to beat down unhindered" might indicate a summer storm has just blown through. The storm itself is not clearly described, but one can make inferences from the information given. Exploring inferences not only helps children improve their reading comprehension, it also helps them explore clues around them in life.

3. Pull the tidbits together. In previous years, your child learned facts about the American and French revolutions. Now it is time to show how events happening on one side of the Atlantic Ocean actually connected to and even impacted events occurring on the opposite side. This is true not only across history, but also in the ways science, history, mathematics, and life in general have coincided through the centuries.

4. The key to this stage is teaching your child how to look beyond facts and learn to make connections, seeing how those facts relate.

In the following pages you will find practical teaching tips and activity suggestions for every concept covered in the placement test. Here are some ways to utilize these tips:

1. Use the suggested activities to strengthen low-scoring areas.

2. For strong areas, focus on activities that will keep your child challenged.

3. At times, having a negative experience with academics can take the joy out of learning. Restore that joy gently by choosing activities that will be fun for your child.

4. Use enrichment activities to put together a "summer camp." This is the perfect time to fill in gaps and bring kids up to grade level.

5. If you are homeschooling, utilize some of these activities on days that are too interrupted or chaotic for the normal school schedule. You can also use them for a relaxed "Friday Fun Day!"

6. Liven up a co-op class by incorporating some of these activities.

PARENT TEACHING TIPS

To use throughout the entire year!

Math

Image of a 100 chart (numbers 1-100) in the top left corner.

WHOLE NUMBERS TO THE BILLIONS

- Practice researching and writing large numbers such as population sizes and statistics.

- Print a 100 chart and begin crossing off or color coding numbers that are divisible by 10, 7, 5, 3, and 2. Only prime numbers should be left.

- Choose two numbers and write out the factors. Now match the common factors and circle the greatest common factor.

- Choose two numbers and write out the multiples. Now match the common multiples and circle the least common multiple.

RATIO AND PERCENT

- Find large groups of objects around the house and practice writing ratios for them.

- Measure a room or a piece of furniture and make a scale drawing of it. Use graph paper to help. You can even rearrange your furniture on paper.

- Look through the sales ads and have your child calculate sale prices based on original price and discount.

- Write the fractions, decimals, and percents on index cards and have your child match them.

FRACTIONS AND DECIMALS

- Print extra worksheets or purchase supplemental workbooks.

- Write fractions and common denominators on index cards and match them.

$$\frac{3}{4} \qquad \frac{2}{8}$$

GEOMETRY

- Practice drawing geometrical shapes.

- Write the types of triangles and their definitions on separate index cards. Match them up.

- Practice cutting irregular shapes and then cutting them into regular shapes and finding the areas.

- Practice using the correct formulas and filling in different numbers.

MULTIPLICATION AND DIVISION

- Print extra worksheets or purchase supplemental workbooks.

- Have your child write his or her own story problems.

JOURNAL YOUR EFFORTS

If you feel that your child is extremely behind, consider formal testing for a learning difficulty such as dyscalculia.

Language Arts

WRITING

- Dictate a piece for your child to write.

- Create a checklist for the writing process and assign due dates for each step if it is a large assignment.

- Discuss a writing assignment with your child before starting. Help him or her plan and gather resources.

- Photocopy a paragraph and cut the sentences apart. Guide your child to put the sentences in a logical order.

SPELLING AND VOCABULARY

- Encourage your child to look up unfamiliar words.

- When correcting your child's writing, ask him or her to find a more specific word in the thesaurus and use it.

- Write prefixes, base words, and suffixes on cards and allow your child to build words.

- Watch your child use the dictionary to correct misspelled words.

LITERATURE

- Make frequent trips to the library

- Continue to read out loud to your child. Consider taking turns reading.

- Join a book club or get a magazine subscription.

- Enjoy a variety of literary genres together.

- Consult several book lists to build your child's personal library.

RESEARCH

- Ask the reference library for a tour of library resources.

- Make up an information scavenger hunt that requires your child to use different library resources.

- Any time your child has a question, write it down and help him or her find the answer next time you are at the library.

- Guide your child to write down where he or she found a piece of information so that it can be retrieved later.

- Practice, practice, practice writing citations.

GRAMMAR AND USAGE

- Write sentences that have grammar and mechanics mistakes in them and lead your child to correct them.

- Purchase some Mad Libs and have some fun with parts of speech.

- Have your child find a passage and list the pronouns and antecedents.

- Write a sentence with missing colons & commas and have your child put them in.

If you feel that your child is extremely behind, consider formal testing for a learning difficulty such as dyslexia or dysgraphia.

History
& Geography

WORLD GEOGRAPHY

- Look up data and information about countries.

- Look at physical maps and political maps side by side to learn why and how people live in different areas.

- Print some maps or get a map workbook or sticker book for extra practice.

- Put a map on the dining room table and cover it with a clear tablecloth.

- Read about historical events from two separate view points such as journal entries or newspapers of the time.

UNITED STATES GEOGRAPHY

- Visit museums as a family.

- Show your child family heirlooms and talk about their history.

- Create a family tree.

- If finances allow, do a DNA test to find your child's heritage.

- Find out about your region's history by visiting the local history section of your library.

WORLD HISTORY

- Choose some exciting historical fiction and biographies to read aloud.

- Talk about how religions have influenced historic events and world culture.

- Try to study events in chronological order, or at least place the events on a timeline to give historical context.

- Find some documentaries on archaeology to learn how we discover the past.

- Look through photographs and paintings of historical events.

UNITED STATES HISTORY

- Discuss why colonists came to America.

- Create an infographic on the three branches of government.

- Read and memorize important political documents and discuss what they mean.

- Create a fictional journal of a favorite time period.

- Encourage family story-telling.

CULTURE

- Choose a historic building or landmark and research it.

- Plan family vacations around historical sites or routes.

- Attend local festivals.

- Encourage your child to choose a historical role model and help him or her do further research.

- Read the newspaper or watch the news together and discuss current events.

JOURNAL YOUR EFFORTS

Science

JOURNAL YOUR EFFORTS

LIVING THINGS

- Enter a science fair.
- Create graphs and charts of weather patterns.
- Show your child how to research a scientific topic at the library.
- Get a microscope and purchase some prepared slides of plant and animal specimens.
- Print pictures of different cells and have your child label them.

PLANTS

- Plant a garden or some potted plants.
- Dissect a flower.
- Visit a state or national park.
- Go for a hike.
- Get a field guide and practice identifying flowers.

CHEMISTRY

- Purchase a chemistry set.
- Get a book about kitchen chemistry from the library.
- Put a periodic table on the dining room table and cover it with a clear tablecloth.

HUMAN BODY

- Purchase some charts or models of the human body.
- Watch some videos about the human body.
- Make a model of the respiratory system with balloons.
- Research consequences of unhealthy lifestyles.

LIFE CYCLES

- Raise some tadpoles or butterflies.
- Grow something on petri dishes.
- Visit a farm or petting zoo at different times of the year.
- Watch a video of a cell dividing.

BIBLE STORIES

- Create a Bible timeline.

- Write some biographical sketches of different Bible characters.

- Find a parallel of the Gospels and read it in chronological order.

- Find information about what was happening at the same time in other areas of the world.

BIBLE PASSAGES

- Read the same passages over and over.

- Mark key words in passages.

- Practice outlining Bible passages.

- Encourage your child to take notes while listening to sermons.

CHURCH HISTORY & MISSIONS

- Read missionary biographies.

- When you study a new country, research missionaries that have served or are currently serving there.

- Get your child involved with a local or foreign missions project.

- Pray for and financially support your church's missionaries.

REFERENCE TOOLS

- Invest in a good Bible dictionary with lots of pictures.

- Choose a word or topic and help your child list all the verses about it.

- Look at biblical maps and then find the modern day locations.

- Practice Bible drills.

THEOLOGY

- Talk about how the blood of a perfect sacrifice was required for the forgiveness of sins.

- Give examples of repentance. Share how God has convicted you.

- Tell your child that only God can keep a covenant perfectly.

- Explain that believers have been purchased out of slavery to sin so that they can become slaves of Christ.

Bible

JOURNAL YOUR EFFORTS

MILESTONES
WHAT TO EXPECT

USING MILESTONES

The timely development of a child is a frequent question and concern among both new and experienced parents. In the following pages you will discover the physical, emotional, and academic development you can expect from your child **by the end of 5th grade**.

The goal of the Well Planned Gal milestones is to have the information on hand as a guideline. These ranges of development can greatly aid you as you parent, teach, and train your child to the next level.

It is important, however, that you do not use these milestones to "diagnose" your child as behind or gifted. It is perfectly normal for children to display a broad range of abilities as they grow and develop.

Many things may influence a child's growth and development, including temporary stress, nutrition, illness, sleep habits, premature birth, learning styles, and physical growth spurts. If you have specific concerns or questions concerning your child's physical or academic progress, we urge you to consult your child's pediatrician.

The Well Planned Gal milestones are outlined in three ranges of growth and maturity.

YOUR CHILD SHOULD BE ABLE TO . . .

This area presents what **most** children this age are comfortable doing. Approximately 80% of children fall into this category.

YOUR CHILD MAY BE ABLE TO . . .

This area presents what **many** children this age are comfortable doing. Approximately 50% of children fall into this category.

YOUR CHILD MAY EVEN TRY TO . . .

This area presents what **some** children this age attempt. Approximately 20% of children -- including gifted or exceptional children -- fall into this category.

Welcome to the wild and crazy middle school years! Not quite a teen, not really a child, your young person is thrust into an exciting time of growth and change. The Beginning to Understand stage usually covers 5th through 8th grade for children ranging in age from 9 to 14. So, as you can imagine, a great deal happens during these years! You can see why it is important, as in every stage, to consider any list of milestones to be a general guideline and not a set of hard, fast rules.

Your child's physical and emotional maturation may happen suddenly in the early years of this stage, or it may slowly dawn over a few years. Some children grow and change steadily while others grow in spurts and then hit plateaus for a while. Regardless, you will likely wake up one day and wonder who the new kid in the house is! Your middle schooler likely feels the same way, one day acting immature and the next trying to be an adult. With patience, knowledge, and love, you both can grow through this transition with a stronger relationship than ever.

As you process through this stage with your child, remember that, although high school is the next step, you have several years to work through these milestones. Beware of comparing him to others, and instead help him identify his unique talents and abilities as you also help him lay a foundation of maturity for the coming stage.

5TH GRADE MILESTONES

Understanding your child's growth

HOW YOUR CHILD IS GROWING

Date	✓	Milestone	Journal
Your child should be able to			
	☐	Demonstrate clear handwriting	
	☐	Become more creative with artwork and crafts	
Your child may be able to			
	☐	Begin developing toward puberty	
	☐	Demonstrate increased independence, including arguing and asserting his opinion	
Your child may even be able to			
	☐	Go through puberty	
How you can help. You can encourage his growth through these milestones with activities like these:			
	☐	Enroll in team sports or supply sports equipment for use with siblings.	
	☐	Provide a special space for personal hygiene items.	
	☐	Give your child specific household responsibilities.	
	☐	Provide craft supplies, idea books, and instructional DVDs	
Notes			

HOW YOUR CHILD IS FEELING

Date	✓	Milestone	Journal
Your child should be able to			
	☐	Have a best friend	
	☐	Converse comfortably with all ages	
	☐	Speak and behave in public with maturity -- at rare times	
Your child may be able to			
	☐	Become more aware of personal appearance and body image	
	☐	Experience sudden mood swings, especially frustration with academics or chores	
Your child may even be able to			
	☐	Think more about the present than about the future	
	☐	Base judgments on definite concepts of right and wrong	
	☐	Desire more privacy	
	☐	Struggle with identity	
	☐	Become opinionated	
	☐	Seek relationships outside of the family	
	☐	Show off	
	☐	Attempt to be more self-sufficient	

	☐	Begin to internalize family values	
	☐	Take more risks	

How you can help. You can encourage his growth through these milestones with activities like these:

	☐	Provide opportunities to participate in deep conversation.	
	☐	Guide him in choosing good friends.	
	☐	Encourage trying new things.	
	☐	Provide a safe place for friends to spend time.	
	☐	Model how to plan ahead.	
	☐	Share stress control techniques.	
	☐	Encourage proper behavior around members of the opposite sex.	

Notes

HOW YOUR CHILD IS LEARNING

Date	✓	Milestone	Journal
Your child should be able to			
	☐	Read longer chapter books for pleasure	
	☐	Write stories	
	☐	Begin long division	
	☐	Convert fractions to decimals	
	☐	Compare metric and American measurements	
	☐	Estimate	
	☐	Draw geometric shapes	
	☐	Write in cursive	
	☐	Write summaries and reports utilizing the writing process	
	☐	Grasp homophones	
	☐	Understand parts of speech and punctuation	
	☐	Identify major mountain ranges and bodies of water	
	☐	Appreciate the importance of a healthy lifestyle	
	☐	Understand atoms	
	☐	Comprehend electricity	
	☐	Identify geologic formations	
	☐	Understand basic meteorology	
Your child may be able to			
	☐	Write reports	

	☐	Correct grammar and mechanics	
	☐	Understand prime numbers	
	☐	Comprehend ratios and percents	
	☐	Multiply with fractions and decimals	
	☐	Solve multi-step word problems	
	☐	Convert units of measurement	
	☐	Find the radius, circumference, and diameter of a circle	
	☐	Understand basic probability and statistics	
	☐	Classify animals	
	☐	Understand how cells work	
	☐	Diagram the structures of plants	
	☐	Comprehend reproduction and life cycles	
	☐	Form a hypotheses and predict multiple outcomes	
	☐	Identify climate zones and major lakes	

Your child may even be able to

	☐	Write a persuasive essay	
	☐	Write a business letter	
	☐	Write a research report	
	☐	Give a speech	
	☐	Study Greek and Latin roots or a modern language	
	☐	Accurately uses troublesome words	
	☐	Identify lines of latitude and longitude	

HOW YOUR CHILD IS LEARNING

Date	✓	Milestone	Journal
	☐	Locate deserts of the world	
	☐	Add and subtract positive and negative numbers	
	☐	Solve ratio and percent problems	
	☐	Divide fractions and decimals	
	☐	Begin pre-algebra and solving problems with one variable	
	☐	Calculate speed and work	
	☐	Understand energy and force	
How you can help. You can encourage his growth through these milestones with activities like these:			
	☐	Memorize poetry.	
	☐	Discuss literature.	
	☐	Write a report.	
	☐	Provide a dictionary or use the reference department of the library.	
	☐	Diagram sentences.	
	☐	Listen to audio books and read aloud.	
	☐	Act out a historical event.	
	☐	Make models.	
	☐	Label maps.	
	☐	Visit civic buildings.	
	☐	Use longitude and latitude to find a location.	
	☐	Calculate basic geometry.	

CPSIA information can be obtained
at www.ICGtesting.com
Printed in the USA
LVHW062219240223
740120LV00001B/9

	☐	Work story problems.	
	☐	Observe animals.	
	☐	Experiment with light.	
	☐	Build a circuit.	
	☐	Visit museums.	
	☐	Listen to different types of instruments and study composers.	
	☐	Attend live concerts.	
	☐	Study cultural art.	

Notes

_____

_____

_____

_____

_____

_____

_____

_____

_____

_____

_____

_____

_____

WELL PLANNED START FEATURES

WHERE DO YOU START?

If your child has finished the 5th grade and you want to make sure they are ready to proceed, this is the book to start with.

If your child is going into the 5th grade, you should test using the 4th grade book; however, you could purchase the 5th grade as a guide for what to cover or expect in the coming year.

If your child is coming out of a school system and you are unsure of where to start or your child's educational experience, there are a few things to consider:

- If your child struggled in 5th grade, start out by giving the 3rd grade test to ascertain any educational gaps. If your child tests well enough to proceed, give the 4th grade test next.

- If your child completed the 5th grade and neither struggled nor excelled, begin with the 4th grade test to ascertain any educational gaps. If your child tests well enough to proceed, give the 5th grade test next.

- If your child excelled in the 5th grade, start with this book and proceed according to the assessment score.

- If your child is special needs, professional diagnostic testing is recommended. If you choose to use Well Planned Start, administer the test using your best judgment while making accommodations for the needs of your child.

EVALUATING ACADEMIC SUCCESS

Created for any family, Well Planned Start allows parents to see exactly where their child is thriving or struggling. The test includes guidelines and instructions to evaluate student proficiency while assessing the exact point of a child's understanding of specific processes, procedures, and information.

The results give the parent a starting point for choosing curriculum or engaging in conversation with teachers to establish a plan for strengthening weak areas.

- Kindergarten - 12th Grade
- Parent Assessment Test
- Student Placement Test
- Includes Bible, History, Science, Math, & Language Arts
- Physical, Emotional, and Academic Milestone Checklists
- Plan of Action Worksheets
- Teaching Tips for Each Subject

ISBN 978-1-942192-90-9

52995

9 781942 192909

$29.95